WANDERINGS IN THE WEALD

BY SHEENA NELSON

123456789

Dedicated to Zoe Warwick and John Collins

I hope it brings back pleasant memories

Kentish Oast house.

Introduction

The garden of England is what Kent is known as and after reading this book you will understand why.

Of course there used to be a lot more industry involving plants such as orchards growing apples, Pears, cherries and cob nuts. Then there were the iconic hop farms with their tell-tale Oasts. Alas most of these wonderful Kentish Oasts have been converted into flats and houses now and the art of growing good beer hops is almost non-existent.

Many Londoners would have their annual 'holiday' hop picking. The children loved being in the countryside for a few weeks enjoying the freedom and getting all the vitamin D they needed for the winter. A whole way of life is now gone as in the late fifties machines took over from people and then imported hops became cheaper and so Kent lost one of its main industries.

Now Kent mainly farms arable food and sheep and grows fruit in huge ancient orchards keeping some of the old varieties going. There are also some vineyards and other local producers of delicious Kentish fare. A lot of the produce can be found in the various farm shops and markets around the Weald.

Tourism is fast becoming the thing for Kent's economy with a working hop farm, blossom tours, many castles, forests, wildlife parks, rare breeds centres, lakes, beaches, art galleries, quaint villages, many footpaths, amazing gardens, Tudor mansions and the channel tunnel all around for people to enjoy and we also have some of the best weather and the most unusual wildlife; what's not to like?

So come with me for a journey through the Kent Weald and see through my photos and prose the stunning magical garden of England.

Cat slide cottages, Great Chart.

Kingsnorth fields, Ashford.

The Weald

Weald is an old English word for wood. Kent was almost covered in forest many years ago. Henry the 8th would go hunting through this forest when visiting his castles here.

Bluebells, Park wood, Ashford

The Kentish woods are a delight all through the year but never so much as in May when the Bluebells come out in abundance.
Walk into a wood and stand and stare! The smell is intoxicating and the view takes your breath away. A carpet of blue as far as the eye can see. It's best to go early in the morning when the dew is still on them so they look fresh especially when taking photos but they look magnificent any time of the day.
Before the bluebells you can find shiny Celandines, Wood Anemones, Wood Sorrel, wild primroses and ferns beginning to unfurl from tight curls into swaying fronds. With the Bluebells comes Stitchwort with its starry white flowers and the tall spires of Pink Campion making a contrast of colours against the fresh green of the leaves.

Stitchwort in the wood.

Summer brings dark canopies above with dappled sunlight pushing through the branches and lighting up the ground and the new growth cathedral like in its height brings welcome shade to all who need it. Speckled Wood butterflies flit around and Bumble bees fly lazily from flower to flower. Look upwards and see patches of deep blue through the thickening tree tops. Rooks caw warnings from up high guarding their precarious nests built on the highest boughs.

Squirrels race up and down tree trunks and jump from one tree to another tails in the air showing off their acrobatics.

Sit in a cool wood on a hot summer's day and you can imagine Faeries and Pixies dancing in glades, perched on flowers and paddling in streams running through the wood bringing essential welcoming water.

The Bluebells are long gone and the ferns are taking over. Brambles grow their spiny branches and insects feed from the flowers and fruit. Here in Kent picturesque dog roses grow; their vintage blooms cascading through the trees and bushes.

Dappled sunlight through the summer trees at Park wood, Ashford.

Autumn arrives and the undergrowth slowly begins to die back apart from the brambles. The leaves change colour and make a wonderful display of reds, oranges and yellows sending the woods into a flame like glory. Kent in autumn is as stunning as in other seasons, autumnal hues abound on every shrub, bush and tree. Squirrels and other hibernating animals get ready their nests collecting food and warm nest linings.

Hothfield in autumn; near Ashford

Penny bun toadstool.

Wander through the woods in autumn and spot the various fungi that seem to appear overnight. Collect sweet chestnuts from their spiny cases for roasting in the cold evenings. Stand on a hill and admire the view when the sun is shining on the autumn leaves turning them into copper and gold glittering beauty.

Winter brings its own rewards of spooky gnarled branches with mosses growing on them. The wood is bare and there's nowhere to hide apart from hollow trees and undergrowth; decaying leaves and wood make homes for beetles and other insects and the leaf mould seeps into the earth to put nutrients back in so that the flora can survive. Berries and seeds are dispersed by birds and the wind so that the woodland will spread. The weak winter sun casts strange shadows and the wood is quiet conserving its energy for the new spring growth.

Hothfield wood in winter with the wild horses.

Fields and Heathlands

Kent is quite flat so the views can be incredible when all you can see are fields and the vast sky for miles. If you do find a hill then the view from the top is often even better as in the view from the Wye nature reserve. It's a must see; it's a panoramic view of the wonderful Kent countryside. You drive through the quaint village of Wye with its lovely branch line station and then up where a crown is carved into the hillside. The Wye crown. It was carved for Edward V11 celebrating his coronation and can be seen from Ashford.

The view across Wye nature reserve.

Wye Crown

SPRING

In spring the fields are beginning to turn green once more and wild flowers start appearing. The grasses grow and the birds look around for nesting material. The animals begin to awaken after their winter sojourn and start looking for food once more.

The sheep have all had their families and lambs gambol around the fields little tails wagging in delight.

Primroses, snowdrops and then daffodils appear here and there spotting the vista with much yearned after colour.

Buds appear on branches and catkins wiggle in the wind. The chestnut trees flourish with 'candles' white and pink standing tall and pretty on branches. Blackthorn show their snowy white little blooms first then The blossom starts to appear everywhere else covering the trees and bushes with wonder. The apple orchards are alight with pink and white shades, cherry trees have a stunning display along with the Magnolia's with their huge waxy blooms.

The whole county is transformed into a spring wonderland. Everywhere you look there seems to be colour and beauty, starry delicate flowers of pink and white, bright green young leaves, darker red leaves of the Cotinus, the yellow of daffodils and dandelions; a rainbow of magical flora painting a gorgeous sunny spring picture across the landscape making you feel glad to be alive.

White cherry blossom

White Dog Rose; Rosa Canina.

Charming cherry blossom.

These cherry trees don't produce edible fruit but are grown for their all year round colour. They grow around the estate where I live. The leaves also change colour through the year so they always look lovely.

Kent Summer

Summer in the garden of England is green. The soil here is rich clay which the trees seem to like as they flourish in the Kent climate. The fields are a riot of shades of green. Huge canopies on the trees, light green new leaves. Darker green leaves on the majestic Oak trees that are dotted around the fields often the only tree standing alone in the centre. The grass in the meadows goes from cream to green to purple and sometimes even blue. Then there's the contrast of the sunny yellow rapeseed adorning field after field shining in the sun.

In June the buttercups appear and cover meadows, hills and fields as far as the eye can see like a golden carpet.

The wildflowers grow among them and on the verges of roads. All the way along some roads there are swathes of Ox-eye daisies, corn poppies etc. and the hedges are made up of willows, their branches billowing in the breeze. Some verges are planted with an array of vintage blooms that hurt the eyes with their beauty.

Wild dog roses cascade down slender branches through the bushes, their pink, red and white blooms glaring out of the greenness.

Majestic Oak at Moat Park, Ashford.

Wildflower verge with buttercup meadow behind; Willesborough Dykes cycle path, Ashford.

Dog roses cascading through the trees with a dragonfly sunbathing.

With the flowers come the insects. There are bees of all varieties; hoverflies, bee flies, butterflies, moths and dragonflies all in a spectrum of colour flying from flower to flower being busy as if they're late like the white rabbit in Alice in wonderland. Other insects scurry by in the undergrowth and spiders weave their webs amongst the grass stalks and lurk in gossamer tunnels waiting for food to come along.

The baby birds have fledged and are practicing their flying techniques and skylarks call from way above the clouds.

Gloriously coloured beetles looking like oil slicks crawl up stalks and perch on petals shining their luminescence to attract females.

The skies over Kent are vast and deep blue making the countryside look tropical. Even on a cloudy, muggy day the air is not oppressive with the huge skies above where the clouds seem to be painted on by Michael Angelo.

There really are not enough adjectives to describe how stunning a summer's day in the Kent countryside is.

Wild flower cycle path, Willesborough Dykes, Ashford

The scenery is incredible here; everywhere you look there are green spaces and flora in abundance; even in the heart of the towns and villages. Hollyhocks grow up through the pavements and scented roses escape over walls. Rosebay willow herb grows in disturbed ground and the beautiful chicory will often be seen in waste ground. Feathery shrubs and low growing bushes adorn the path edges and wild verges where snakes hide are kept wild but managed by Kent wildlife trust. Hawks can be seen hovering in the sky eyeing up their dinner from afar. Such urban beauty has rarely been seen in other towns and I feel privileged to live in such a place as this with the amount of conservation that goes on all through the year, thoughtfully and tastefully planned out so that the paths and estates see colour in every season, sometimes it seems as though the scenery changes every week and the eyes never get bored.

Gorgeous Hollyhocks.

The brightness of summer is ending now, it's September and years ago the time when the hops would be ripe and people from London would come down to pick them and have a hard but fabulous time in their hop shacks. The women would make them homely and they would all cook on a communal fire, like camping out. The kids would run wild and free and go home as fit as fleas. They also got a good night's sleep by making hop pillows as hops are soporific as well as the families being exhausted after hard graft in the fields getting bitter, stained hands.

It's sad to think an industry as big as hop growing has almost disappeared now and the hop huts are either gone or turned into holiday cottages and the Oast farms are now flats and houses that only the very rich can afford. The scenery is a lot poorer without towering poles of vines and yellowing hops hanging from them.

The leaves are gradually changing colour and falling. Animals are collecting bedding for their winter hibernation and the weald is full of free food for them to hoard in their nests. Berries and nuts ripen and mushrooms and toadstools spurt up from the forest floor.

The weald has a spectacular display of autumnal colours everywhere you look; a delightful palette of reds and oranges and from brown to yellow. The countryside is quieter now and things slow down. Mists appear showing up the many intricate cobwebs in a stunning display across the bushes.

There are many fruits and nuts available including the Kent cob nut which is delicious and can be found growing wild along with succulent blackberries and elderberries.

The harvest is in; the fields are now bare apart from stubble and the hedgerows which are growing berries.

People and wildlife are in their element now with so much free food available and such a variety, autumn is a wonderful harvest time. Nuts to store, berries for birds and blackberries for jam along with hard tasty pears and apples of so many varieties for pies and cider. There are Onions to pickle, jams to make, marrows for chutney and of course pumpkins for Halloween and pumpkin pie and soup. Try drying the seeds, they're very good for you and you can also plant some the next spring.

Autumn the time of plenty.

August scene in Little Chart

Harvesting the apples.

Kent has many apple orchards; some are ancient varieties, some newer ones. Some also grow pears and other fruits for farm shops and greengrocers. It's a labour of love from spring to autumn, from blossoms to fruit and the delight of eating an apple not long picked from the tree. You can also go legal scrumping here as there are many wild apple trees; some escapees from orchards and a lot along the roadsides are from people throwing apple cores out of car windows. Look closely and it shouldn't take long to spot one.

Wild highland bull on Hothfield common.

The highland cattle roam free along with the wild polish horses across Hothfield common. It's lovely to roam among them and watch them grazing. They help manage the heathland and woodland there and they are a wonderful sight merging in with the prehistoric landscape. Walk round and see if you can spot them.

Autumn; the time of mists and mellow sheep; Shadowhurst.

Kent mainly farms sheep although there are also cows around. Sheep are plentiful here and are part of the landscape, especially Romney marsh sheep that are a native variety, very hardy to enable them to survive harsh winters on the chilly marshes. The lamb apparently is delicious. (I wouldn't know as I'm a vegetarian). In early spring the lambs appear frolicking and wagging their little tails, happy to be free to play.

Winter in wonderland.

Winter here is magical also especially when there is a hoar frost or snow. The landscape is transformed into a sparkling wonderland full of glitter. Abstract patterns form on icy puddles and cow parsley looks like lace. The trees are transformed into shining silver although the birches already are of course and there are a lot of those around; their startling bark adding to the beauty.

Birds cry overhead echoing in the stillness of the day and reeds and rushes stiff like stalagmites adorn the edges of lakes, ponds and frosty rivers. The water birds learn to ice skate searching for water and the low sun sends diamond sparkles across the lake.

The views are amazing with the deep blue of the sky contrasting with the whiteness.

Of course it also rains and there are just dull days but get your wellies on, kick the leaves and splash in the puddles to keep warm. There is still lots of fun to be had in the Kentish winter Weald.

The wild horses of Hothfield

The fields at Hothfield on a frosty day.

Churches

There are many churches to view in Kent; most are ancient some from the 12thC. Monasteries are usually in ruins though as Henry 8th destroyed them in his haste to abolish the catholic faith.

The churches though are varied and have round, conical and square towers. The graveyards are decked out with the most glorious yew trees, gnarled, ancient, knotted and tangled, branches twisting through the years. Mind them though as they are poisonous. Yew trees have many stories to tell; from pagans to Christians, the trees have been sacred. Look closely at the multi-coloured bark and how the sturdy branches entangle themselves. Horse chestnut trees also grow in abundance here with their firework like candle blossoms and then the fruit picked for children to play conkers; not to be mistaken for sweet chestnuts that grow in forests, the nuts of those are very tasty cooked on a real fire.

The churches often have murals painted with medieval hand and plaques celebrating family life and knights of yore. Stained glass sparkles in the sun lighting the dimness and sending dust motes flying.

Mostly I like the serenity a church brings, there's always something peaceful there as if the modern world stops at the door.

Yew tree.

Hothfield church in winter sun.

St Peter & St Paul church, Appledore.

St Mary's church, Great Chart

St Mary's Ancient church at Sevington.

Lakes, rivers, moats and ponds.

Water is also a big part of the Weald. There are ponds in woods and streams, lakes to walk round, little waterfalls to gaze at, the river Stour and the Royal military canal, built to protect Kent in the Napoleonic wars but never used for its purpose.

The canal is 28 miles long and goes from Seabrook to Cliffsend. Today it is a clean and wonderful place to walk, or kayak down. You can like I do; do small bits at a time. Any time of year the canal looks lovely but in the summer there are striking yellow water lilies and plenty of dragonflies, butterflies and beetles. Ducks and swans paddle around and coots and moorhens call from the rushes and reeds. The canal has wonderful views across farmland, fields, meadows and villages.

The RMC at Hamstreet.

Lakes and ponds.

Singleton Lake, Ashford.

Singleton Lake is a man-made lake, dug out in the 1970's for the public to walk round and fish in. Also for the wildlife which since it was made has become prolific. There are plenty of Canada geese, greylag geese, swans, coots, moorhens and ducks but also you can if lucky see Kingfishers, Grebe's, Egrets and Black headed gulls.

In the trees Siskins and blue tits abound along with the Robin, Blackbirds, sparrows etc. I am yet to see the kingfisher or a Heron so I have to keep going back around this stunning lake. You can walk all the way round, the paths are well laid and wheelchairs could get round but it might be a bumpy ride! It's not a long way round; just right for a stroll. There is a footpath that goes to Great Chart and also to Victoria Park through the Watercress fields, water meadow walk.

Opposite the lake is Buxford mill meadow where there is a small pond and at the top there is woodland with a stream and parts of the old mill workings. The wood looks prehistoric with the water lying round the tree trunks like Mangroves.

The mill is now a private house.

There is so much to do around the lake and fields. You can fish there but need a ticket from the council. There is also a circular walk through Buxford mill wood back round to the lake. Parking is either opposite the meadow or further down the lane there is a large car park, nice for picnics. It is one of my favourite places in Ashford for walking along with Hothfield common.

Egret taken in Buxford meadow.

Canada geese on Singleton lake.

Beaches.

The beaches are not really part of th
e Weald but are worth a mention.

The beaches around Kent are very clean and have a great atmosphere whether you want an original setting with sand, fairground and kiss me quick hats as at Margate or a more atmospheric quiet pebbly beach such as Dymchurch. There are wooden groins lined up looking out to sea and pools left by the tide await gulls scavenging for food.

You can see for miles along most of the coastlines from the white cliffs of Dover to the flatness of Hythe, the views are incredible. Imagine the pilots during WW2 seeing those cliffs and knowing they were nearly home, what a welcoming sight!

There are a lot of museums and places of interest concerning the wars around Kent as it is the closest county to France and therefore a lot of the armed forces were stationed here; all worth visiting as a reminder of the sacrifices the men and women made for our freedom.

Head to Whitstable for the oysters and amazing sunsets and to Deal for Walmer castle; Sandgate where George Orwell once lived and Dungeness for desert like scenery and a large nature reserve.

It is the North Sea though so it is quite chilly.

I prefer the beaches in winter when you can don your wellies and wander across the sand or stones in relative peace watching the glorious sea birds that over winter here. Don't forget your camera for rare shots.

Some beaches like Camber sands allow horses on them and it's always a lovely scene seeing them trotting along the breakwater.

Margate has Dreamland funfair, recently reopened and the Turner art gallery on the harbour which is well worth a visit.

Whitstable has an oyster festival in the summer, pop over and taste their famous fare. Nip to Tankerton and see the colourful beach huts lining the front. A visit to Sandwich is a must even if it's just a photo opportunity for the signpost which reads Ham Sandwich. Deal and Dover have castles to explore. From Folkestone to Dungeness is one long promenaded walk including lovely Hythe where there is a steam railway and Dymchurch with its Mortello tower in the car park. Dungeness is a nature reserve and a nuclear power station, bleak but beautiful. Then down through Camber into Sussex with Rye historical harbour, Winchelsea atmospheric beach along to Hastings and Brighton. No two beaches the same and each one having its own merits.

Hythe looking towards Sandgate.

Delightful Dymchurch

The White cliffs of Dover.

Villages

If you like all things historical or just like stunning beauty then look no further than a Wealden village. Each one has its own beauty, with Tudor, weather board and cat slide tiled cottages or converted Oast houses with cottage gardens and trees and shrubs along every street.

It's like stepping back in time to when the world was slower apart from all the modern cars that are parked everywhere. I imagine the streets and lanes when only horses were used as transport; it's not difficult looking down these ancient byways. In the summer Hollyhocks grow out of the pavements, a truly gorgeous sight along with oriental poppies and purple foxgloves that grow in wild areas.

The Tudor buildings are incredible with their pied features, some bent out of shape over the centuries. Some of them are almost mansions and some are quaint cottages but all have stood the test of time and if only they could speak we would have history lessons galore.

Some modernisation can be seen as in village shops with adverts for the lottery and two cars outside each house. The sad part of these times is when front gardens are paved over to make car ports.

There are some new builds but they are done sympathetically and after a while they weather and look older.

There's Pluckley with its arched windows that the Dering family had put in every house on their estate considering them lucky as one of their ancestors escaped out of one. Pluckley is also one of the most haunted villages in England and where some of the darling buds of May series was filmed

Then there's Smarden which is full of stunning houses and Tudor cottages looking over the churchyard. There's Appledore which is a wonderful village with a very long main road with little shops along it and a lovely quaint tea shop. There are Hollyhocks growing through the pavements here.

Then there's Rolvenden with its converted Oast houses and huge Tudor piles.

Then we have the confusing dens, Biddenden, Bethersden and Benenden, all lovely in their own right and all close to one another. They all have plenty of Tudor buildings, great old pubs, lovely shops and good restaurants.

Sissinghurst is gorgeous with its gardens and former residence of Vita Sackville-West which is open to the public.

Cranbrook is a big village with a working windmill and there are also windmills at Woodchurch and Willesborough. Woodchurch has a rare breed's centre which is well worth a visit and a quintessential village green. There is also Goudhurst with its ancient Tudor pub, independent shops and a lovely stone church that glows warmly in the sun. There is a village pond here with resident ducks.

So those are a few of the amazing villages that adorn the countryside in the Weald.

Each stunningly quaint village is like a scene from a Miss Marple episode. There are far too many points of interest and words of praise for these amazingly well preserved jewels of England so the best thing to do is to go and see them for yourself.

Woodchurch windmill.

The haunted Black horse pub at Pluckley with the Dering arched windows.

Pluckley was used in the Darling buds of May series, the farm they used is called Buss farm near Bethersden which is now a private farm with holiday lets and it has a car show every July; Pluckley is said to be one of the most haunted villages in England. Go for a walk in the screaming woods if you dare!

Smarden churchyard houses.

The other side of the M20 are roads to Canterbury and the north which take you through some fabulous scenery.

There are more stunning villages here; you have the three c's Charing, Challock and Chillham which are more or less all on the A252. Each has its own charm. Charing has a quaint main street with some good shops and amazing old houses. There are also the remains of one of the Bishops palaces by the church. Challock on the crossroads has Kingswood forest, an enormous acreage of woods and fields with a huge variety of trees. Chillham village lies on a hill and is a small but scenic Tudor village with a large church. There is also a stately home there called Chillham castle. Then there is Boughton Aluph with its typical English village green and Eastwell manor that is now a high class hotel.

Charing Bishops palace, the old with the new.

Along the A28 at Bilting there is a fabulous farm shop called Perry Court farm. They grow a lot of their own produce and each harvest time they have a big apple festival with many things going on. It's a great place to stock up on your five a day goods.

Perry Court farm apples

Tudor houses at Chillham.

These pictures are just a dip in the ocean to what you can see if you drive round Kent and you will never forget the experience. If you love history and nature there is no better place to be. Kent is also warm as it's nearer to France than other counties. We have fine rain here, plenty of blue skies and although the soil is clay plants thrive here. We also get some unusual flora and fauna that make their way across the channel. Kent is a very interesting county and really should not be missed.

Frosty Tudor house, Godington.

Towns

There are but a few major towns in the Weald of Kent. One such place is Tenterden, yes another den which actually means pasture usually for pigs. Tenterden is a busy small town in the middle of the Weald with a long high street full of shops both national and independent. There are good visitor attractions here; The Kent and East Sussex steam railway is here with its 10.5 mile track to Bothiam where there is a castle. They have events there such as Thomas the tank engine visits and WW2 weekends. There is also a museum, a leisure centre and Smallhythe place, the home to Ellen Terry. Tenterden is surrounded by weald villages.

Ashford the town where I live is the gateway to Europe where you can catch the high speed train to the Chunnel. It goes from London to Folkestone but Ashford has the international station which is an amazing design, 50's space age does 30's art deco.

Then there is the outlet where one can buy designer gear at cheap prices but it is a blot on the landscape with its bright orange and white tent like structure towering over the land, an eyesore Ashford could do without and is certainly not in keeping with the rest of the town. Ashford although quite big still has old parts and preserved places. It has many parks including Victoria Park with its wonderful fountain and Queen Mum Park with two rivers and plenty of walkways, cycle paths and fields among which are copses of mixed trees. Ashford has a good shopping centre, plenty of parking and a swimming pool/leisure complex. It is divided into boroughs; Stanhope, Singleton, Willesborough and Kingsnorth. Each borough is different. Willesborough has the windmill and is spread wide; Stanhope is more urban; Singleton is lovely and green and has a large lake with leafy roads and pleasant estates; finally kingsnorth which is the nicest borough in my opinion, probably because I live there. It is like being in the middle of the countryside so well has it been planned. The roads are all full of shrubs either side of the paths which have cycle paths on them and the estate is mainly flat. There is a lovely park with a moat where you can go fishing. It has three playgrounds and a footpath down to Tesco which is at the end of Park Farm. There are two quite large woods, one near the park and the other one further down the estate by a school. Behind all this there are numerous fields where people take their dogs or just go walking. Then there is a playing field and Kingsnorth church. Along Sheepsfold lane there is a new cycle path called willesborough Dykes that leads to Asda and the outlet. There are hundreds of wildflowers planted along the path which look absolutely stunning in June. There are so many footpaths and walks here; you can never get bored of it. Get on your bike and cycle for miles round the estates and fields which have well kept paths.

All in all I think all other towns and cities should be like Ashford and be greener; it's a beautiful place to live.

There is a lot to do here in Ashford. As well as large parks there is a leisure centre, health centres, a cinema complex, bowling, both lawn and indoor, a library, cycle paths, the outlet and other shops, a big market at the weekends, a gym, various hobby clubs and a bingo hall among other fun things like skate parks and many footpaths. There are also nice pubs, nightclubs and good restaurants not to mention the wonderful countryside in and around it.

The Hubert Fountain, Victoria Park, Ashford.

There is a whole load of exciting things to do in the areas surrounding the Weald. Forests, castles, gardens, hop farms, lakes, water sports, steam trains, guided tours and walks, windmills, antique shops, car boot sales and sightseeing tours and trails. You can learn all about H.E. Bates, Dickens, Turner and H.G. Wells who all lived here at some time. Further afield there is Canterbury with its magnificent Cathedral, Rochester with its castle and a wonderful large bookshop. Chatham dockyard where Call the midwife and many other things are filmed, an historic dockyard living museum. The national trust and English Heritage have many houses, castles like Hever and Leeds and also many gardens to visit; far too many to list but you will surely never be bored either living here or on being holiday.

Willesborough Dykes cycle path with the designer outlet.

Kent; wonderful scenery, incredible adventures, unforgettable memories.

My garden of England.

Sparrowhawk in my garden.

Goodbye for now.

Blue moon. Daylight moon in a stunningly blue Kentish sky.

Dover Harbour; next stop France. Swimming there is also an option.

USEFUL WEBSITES AND OTHER PLACES OF INTEREST.

Visitkent.co.uk

Tenterdentown.co.uk

The Kent and East Sussex railway.

Visittheweald.co.uk

Kentwildlifetrust.org.uk

Kent life magazine

Kent county council

Kent.gov.uk

English heritage

National trust

Greensands way

Ashford borough council

Kent downs area of outstanding natural beauty.

Ordnance survey maps

CHECK OUT MY OTHER BOOKS ALL AVAILABLE ON AMAZON AND KINDLE.